OF ORACLES
AND MONSTERS

Poems by
J. P. Dancing Bear

GLASS LYRE PRESS

Copyright © 2019 J. P. Dancing Bear
Paperback ISBN: 978-1-941783-

All rights reserved: Except for the purpose of quoting brief passages for review, no part of this book may be reproduced or transmitted in any form or by any means, electronic or mechanical, including photocopying, recording, or by any information storage and retrieval system, without permission in writing from the publisher.

Design & Layout: Steven Asmussen
Cover Art:
Copyediting: Elizabeth Nichols

Glass Lyre Press, LLC
P.O. Box 2693
Glenview, IL 60025
www.GlassLyrePress.com

OF ORACLES AND MONSTERS

Contents

I BECAME THE THING

Oracle of Trophonius	1

ALREADY FORGOTTEN

Early Warning System	5
Oracle of Rust	6
Inward Oracle	7
Oracles of Vanity	8
Oracle of the Cut	9
My Father as Oracle	10
Oracle with Black Butterflies	11
Oracle of the Virga Fields	13
Oracle of Seed	14
The Oracle of Garbage	15
Blind Oracles with Birds	17
The Oracle of Article Five	19
Oracle with Flamingo Companion	20
The Small People	22

GOLD-PLATED PROMISES

The Oracle of Failure	25
Rural Oracles	27
The Oracle of Warranties	29
Hillary Clinton as Cassandra	31
Oracle of *Entertainment Tonight*	32

LOST ALL SENSE

Hole	35
Oracle of Obstruction	37
Oracle of Collusion	38
Preexisting	40
Oracle of Confederate Statues	43
There was Time for One More Racial Slur In Ceremony to Honor the Last Code Talkers	45
The Oracle of Tender Shelters	47
Remember	48
Manifestly Unqualified	49
Oracle of the Wounded Earth	50
After School Special (with Armed Teachers)	52
Nationalism	54
The Oracle of America First	55
Oracle of Tribalism	56
Oracle of Witch Hunts	57
Dear Jeff	58
Homunculus	59
Adam West	64
Fractured Lullaby in a Zinke Landscape	65
How to Build a Monster	66
Who Knew?	68
The Oracle of Liar, Liar	69
Landscape with the Fall of Icarus	71
"...The Stirring, Unmistakable Patriotism of the Velociraptor..."	72

YOU WILL KNOW SMOKE

Autumnal Oracle	75
Oracle of The Late Waking	76
Oracles' End	78
Blind Prophets	79
Gacela of Patriotic Traitors	80
Oracle of Plutonion	81
The Last Vision of Cassandra	82
Great—Again	83
Oracle of Recurring Oracles	85
Acknowledgments	89

I BECAME
THE THING

Oracle of Trophonius

Body of hunches and blood-colored robes, body of denied desires,
I lowered myself into the oracle's mouth where she rose
from her pool of tears. Voice of black trees, voice of valley
light, whispering a worm of quiet spells that chilled and warmed
the old flesh. Somewhere, I stopped wishing for the changes
of others, ceased to need their transformations as a means
of making myself content. I was no more happier with this shift
for I became the thing that needed reshaping.

•

I walked the mists and fogs of doubt, I drank in the watery moon,
but saw no shade or light that was my own. Why is it we want
to move the boulders within the caves of ourselves, stones most
will never see? She was rising up to the surface, she was rising
to spit me out into a fever dream. I ranted and wandered, homeless,
and begging—not for the charity of others, but for a kindness in myself.

ALREADY FORGOTTEN

Early Warning System

You brush away the sand
to find the words underneath
in an unfamiliar hand
in an unfamiliar tongue.
You study them
thinking they might be
a warning or a history
of warnings or a lament
for love—a love of humans
who are so delicate in this world
as to think they can change it.

Oracle of Rust

Let me bathe in the sweet rust of lies, in the trickle-
voice of old leaks and seeps of ground water. I
love to feel each word well up and vine, snake around
my limbs, my torso, like the arms of a lover I know better
than to let near. The old gods look into you, see the thing
wriggling within and what they riddle you to, is this root
where that which is beckoned calls, that little flush
of old browning blood, that smear of vision, *look*, they say:

•

*even if you find a god that will have you, there's still so much
confessing for you to do.* Then they make me breathe
the vapors and the fumes of forgetting, they make me
fall into the stubble field of our collected griefs, ground
cracking, aching for tears, they make me fall to my knees
so you might know the ways I have already forgotten.

Inward Oracle

"THERE'S A DONALD TRUMP IN ALL OF US."—CHRIS HAYES

Apollo, Apollo my old ray of truth, only because
of the harnessed sun, not the shadow cast—the lie.
Everyone comes to me for something they want—
answers to the whens, the wherefores, the where arts,
when the heart is the future of a dormant volcano
at the foot of which you might live your entire life
in peace and content, still you only want to know
of the violence, the screaming, the catastrophe.

•

The old kings are good for provoking the gods, adding
to your fear—dwell upon eruptions and greed. The eye
boils in such futures, mad monarchs laugh, they clutch
their scepters in gloom and this your consumed, scorched
heart spent on a fork, in an unopened alleyway. Each ray
offers a silhouette, a child's lie, obvious only when focused on.

Oracles of Vanity

Don't be silly, only nothing sees nothing, because everything
is in the act of seeing itself. The future is a catwalk where
the body flounces several gauzy colors, round after round
until the consuming self picks a fabric, possibilities, potentials,
the kinetic energy locked in a cell, the chemical processes
of a devourer's life: entropy: breaking: dividing: cuts: slices,
sections: cleaves: slit: tear: fragment: piece: parse: bite: byte:
bit: one: zero: on: off: proton: electron: lepton: dark matter.

•

When Macbeth's three witches Brailled their palms along
the Pacific Rim, they dreamed they wore rings of fire. Does
the outward eye completely boil away to reveal the basin
of a brilliant future? Or an insufferable desert? Where the missing
consume the soul—a collapsed star; a beacon for strange attractors.
I felt attraction once and have regretted the results ever since.

Oracle of the Cut

Here is the cut of light
I hold in my hands

hundreds of twilights
intersect and diverge

I saw the bombs flare
windows disintegrated

edges and shards
deep into my heart

my vision slice I cried
everyone else said

good morning
or good night

My Father as Oracle

Answer me this Father: As you stood in your planted field,
as the first hail smashed the ground, as the twister tore
and writhed, when you saw it all reflected in your lake,
did you see a different life for yourself? What do you think
gets ruined first, now? Behind you, a shingle lifts from the roof
like a single prophetic leaf. The stoic face of my dad, wind
pushing his fading hair around. Come on, Dad, decide what
you'd like to go back and change—make a different outcome.

•

The way you tell it, you lived a lifetime in the root cellar, in
the darkness, cracks of light as boards were bowed but held.
You and the space where carrots and potatoes were to be held
while outside those roots of the future were pounded by fists
of sudden ice. Now that you are dead and have no use for it,
tell me, tell me everything I don't know about regret yet.

Oracle with Black Butterflies

I think it's time you understand something:

each future peered into is burning—

the present mass meeting itself

through time and a tear in space.

You may not feel the quantum heat

because it is in several places all at once.

I was once a singer

and will be again

my throat full of flames,

my hair blending with wild dry grass—

and did I mention the black hole butterflies?

They are everywhere, at once, like my eyes,

smoldering beautifully.

When one lands it turns to ash

though it still carries its natural disasters

under wing—

a song in the wind,

smoke in my ears

and a close sun melting what's left

of our polar ice.

We are all pretending

that we are not the spark and the flame

that the world burns

despite our best efforts—

this is the lie we weave into our lullabies.

The breath under our prayers

at the edge of our nightly beds:

please, god, don't wake me to my own guilt.

Oracle of the Virga Fields

In the silence of the day you can ask yourself if you know where
the music of the world comes from. Is it the virga that looks
like clouds dragging strings across the sky? Is it the tight lines
between the ghosts of telephone poles? All those voices trapped
inside twisting wires, humming in transformer boxes, mingling
with the whine of insects filling the fields. Even way out here, on empty
roads that connect empty towns—where heat rises watery
like reverse virga, you can hear the origins of a choral coming together.

•

These fields have seen too much future, too much progress, not
to have a song. They still hold a memory of trees rooting deep into
the ground. They remember being unfenced, how their animal souls moved
freely through the land. You can see them now and again, sad eyes
looking for something gone, something removed—they stalk the scars
of asphalt and moan something raw and very close to prayer.

Oracle of Seed

In my vision, I lay my face onto the surface of vision,
not as a dreamer or as some eavesdropper but because
my face must meet my other face and see with extra eyes,
breath with an extra nose and mouth. The flowers shall be
my ears, the tendrils shall stretch into the future, I will smell
evaporation as one more alternative collapses, as others condense
into this reality. Everyone says they would like to see the future
but without cost to themselves, therefore I am here

   •

                 but also there.
I am in two places at the same time: Summer fruit and Autumn
withering. When I speak, people only hear what they want,
like items on a shopping list: wild berries—not seeds; peace
without the ensuing preamble of war; love without all the losses;
a new place to call home though some will see as a prison cell.

The Oracle of Garbage

I can never apologize enough, never reach the threshold

    of my own forgiveness

  the rib cage is a reminder

    of the jailed heart

      I've seen the world die—true

many times and by our carelessness, our cavalier

    disregard for life

I've witnessed all the readings of the word "dominion"

    and the petty who exploit

  whatever the gods give, take the scale

    whenever the inch is given

the smallness, the meaninglessness, the box of imps

    we keep within our minds

      is our end—even if

    one of us chooses to resist, chooses the many

      someone else cannot see

    the inclusive heart, the collective soul

          —last sigh of extinction

      the tired body falls and decays, like our cities

      here we have erected another garbage dump

        out there an island of trash

heart-shaped

          and poisonous

    why do I look into the future, you ask?

   Why does one hold onto a discarded and frayed rope—

        count each thread before it disintegrates?

Because one of us is always doomed to hope.

Blind Oracles with Birds

We feel the surface of our pages

                more than read them

        we are the broken wings

           of common sparrows

    or at least that's what I think the pages say

          and in my picked-apart heart

                  this sounds like truth.

My sister, I think, is crying

          perhaps out of joy

    because she hears it too—

                the chitter of beaks
          the scratching of their feet nearby.

We keep moving our hands over paper wings,

    over each other's fingers;

and I whisper a lullaby for the long hall of our future,

        for the long haul

    of withering environments.

The birds know there are answers in this library

    just as we imagine words
    must exist on these pages

even though we are blind

      and birds cannot read

and the floorboards we sit upon

    are worn to splinters

which we think indicates once there were a lot of people here

    opening books and looking for answers

and now my sister says there are so many ghosts here.

We guess they found their answers

      like good dust jackets, they fall
      like tatters and ash.

The Oracle of Article Five

Everyone believes they are innocent
—so pure as to open
the Arc of the Covenant
or take a peek inside Pandora's Box

Or to wonder why the Lady of the Lake
doesn't hand out swords to everyone...

Some among us even know the history of the devil

but make the deal anyway.

You don't need me
to tell you what you already know

You don't need me
to tell you how you and you entire family are enslaved

You won't need me
to tell you *I told you so*

though I already did.

Oracle with Flamingo Companion

> ... LISTEN: THERE'S A HELL
> OF A GOOD UNIVERSE NEXT DOOR: LET'S GO
> —E. E. CUMMINGS

When you are a flamingo there is no talking to you—

go ahead and S your neck

ruffle your feathers—I can

feel your eyes burning into my back;

still I keep my vigil on the world beyond this one,

where you and I are once again

the old lovers we had always been

and you are

anything but bright plumage and mad stares.

Yes, I am angry with you,

because you would stay in this world

falling as heavy as an eyelid near deadly sleep.

Because one universe over the sun is rising

and we are not

bathed in sunset

and you stand next to me

not knee-deep in water

not bright pink

but on two feet and with your lovely arms

locked with mine.

One universe over

falling like a single flaming feather

the air so pure

we forget to breathe,

we forget

this world in its flames.

The Small People

Small people were getting into the hard places.
Like dust, they were coming in through tight openings,
through windows and doors ajar, on the bottoms of our feet,
landing in the corners, under the couch, behind books.

I believed in cleansers, in filters, in the power
of the vacuum and the scrub. ...At least on Sundays.
Righteously bright surfaces, rugs beaten in the sun,
mops, brooms, rags, brushes sweeping the rooms.

They come in from the fields, from their labors.
Those people who had studied me, so privileged in my walk
to the kitchen from the living room. They knew me,
my moods, my habits, things I never thought to share.

I, I never knew they were there. Are there still.

How can I not do things differently now?

GOLD-PLATED PROMISES

The Oracle of Failure

> "WE'RE WATCHING A GENERATION GROW UP
> WHO DOESN'T KNOW HOW TO FAIL."
> —ANDY BRANER

Deep within the cracks of the earth
Pools of water in caves
Taking but not reflecting light,

Here the human tears are gathered
With their fears, the black psychology
Of denial and blame

The stench of sulfur and gas fills the air
It waits for the music of scapegoats

It waits in a black self-hatred.

Lyrics of layoffs,
fight songs for isolationists,
anthems of asylum denials,
dirges for the xenophobes—

Go back to...
Love it or leave it...
Lock them up...
Death to...

The matchhead loves
Everything flammable

It's flame is all that matters—
Can it be bigger?
Can it destroy?
Can it burn a planet?
Be its own star?

If you are an arsonist, do you not dream of Hell?

The matchhead loves its violence.
The matchhead thinks only of itself.
The matchhead dreams it can purify.

What is failure then?

It is the heart of a people in denial.

Self-inflicted ignorance.
Laziness. Refusal
of responsibility.
Coveting the fruits of another's labor.
Open thievery.

Be the victim is an excuse.
Be the victim is our gameshow theme song anthem.

Rural Oracles

On Sundays the idea was to sit down
at the table with our offerings

but it was always a mess—
one of us falling into a trance, staring
into an opening only they saw, all-
the-while letting plates slip, pouring milk
past the thirsty lip of a glass—

 this is where I see you, yes,
you, of the thousand eyes, an Argus Arbus
taking pictures, capturing the wild
soul
      we will haunt you
our prairie ghosts of moments
our half-eaten dinners
our *Sundee* bests.

There is always fire hiding in the sea
of grass, the miles and hours of potential
violence—we daughters of hail,
of lightning
of howling tornadoes.

We never judge your future
as you judge our present and past.

Yes, we knew carpetbaggers would
come, all big city rich, gold-plated
promises of better crop yields,
the men no longer needing to take their own
lives to pay the bank.
Even when we could not see
this future, we wanted it
more than most.
So we forgot ourselves, our histories,
and voted to ignore
even our own visions—the foreclosures,
the trade war, our crops rotting in the fields,
the rust and dust of campaign promises.

Instead we went on
forgetting—

Out back our mother's spirit
Is white sheet torn
from its dry line
galloping the plains
and some of us are sad for it,
some of us envy her—no longer
worried about the decreasing
market value of the land.

That freedom to sway
like a golden stalk, just
before the first sizzle of change

in our weather.

The Oracle of Warranties

"DUH! WINNING!" —CHARLIE SHEEN

Everyone will tell you to take responsibility

for your actions

and your inactions

but I've seen what happens

the punishments and sentences

who does the right thing?

In baseball the saying goes: "if you're not cheating

you're not trying hard enough."

Why don't we live like utility players?

Why not cut-up and dishonor the contracts

of society?

Like here there are a lot of killers,

we have a lot of killers—

we are like a nation of killers.

You think we're so innocent?

They came to me with illegal information

—who wouldn't use this?

What am I a Boy Scout?

No. I hire boy scouts to make me look good.

I told you everything

you ever wanted to hear—

sold it to you *buyer beware*.

So don't come back now

crying about the fake warranty.

I could see all of you coming!

I closed up shop,

I moved beyond the border wall

to a state with no extradition

and the loveliest nesting dolls

—you might care to look me up—

we could make a deal!

I know people

who know people.

Hillary Clinton as Cassandra

"...HE'D (PUTIN) RATHER HAVE A PUPPET AS THE PRESIDENT
OF THE UNITED STATES... AND IT'S PRETTY CLEAR..."

It's never enough to see the strings and the hands move,
both the small wooden replica and the human,
the doll jaw jut forward, the lips purse
as if to suck a straw of faux soda. What is anger,
real anger, is represented in the carved scowl,
Geppetto's attempt to put a remembrance
of boyhood rouging, of emotion, into the rendition.

But it all smears into a apocalyptic orange
that is ominous and obvious and overlooked.
For what is hope, if not to ignore the klaxons
and open one's arms to doom while desiring
a different future? This is where the salesman
beats your heart, and says it is his own.

Each minute the oracle feels time slipping into reality.
She is pelted with the words Cassandra knows too well:
"lock her up"—Sad and ironic as gold plate on rust,
as the drip and seep of corners cut in construction.
Out the cell window of the soul, one can see the republic
in full blaze, one can see it as she's seen it for decades,
and her vision of herself, helpless to stop the people
she serves and dies for, from themselves and their strung emperor
a painted reflection, who mirrors another's heart
where his own might have been.

Oracle of *Entertainment Tonight*

It's time you stop electing people who call themselves
big stars and brag

about all the things only a star can do.

All they want is a *mirror, mirror on the wall*
and not a smart-assed one either,

but a beautiful sycophant

who says, *My god you
look stunning today!*

and encourages you to belittle the comets
the binary twins, the dull dwarves
and anything science might suggest is more
interesting than these
finite sparks
who do their best to redefine
what we think is attractive.

For a dollar I'd pay you to change the channel

—it adds up, you know—

watch *Cosmos*
learn not to be tricked by pulsars,
false beacons,
or drawn to the event horizon
to be consumed
so insignificantly, so thoughtlessly,
learn to recognize the signs,
the real and metaphorical red flags.

It's time you understand
fame and begin
to see the attraction

is only one way.

LOST ALL SENSE

Hole

> THERE ARE 2 TRUTHS ABOUT LITTLE DONNIE AND ONLY 2: THAT HE WILL DO
> ANYTHING FOR MONEY REGARDLESS OF WHO OR WHAT IT HURTS; AND THE HOLE
> LEFT IN HIS SOUL FROM A MOTHER AND FATHER THAT HAD NO USE FOR HIM
> WILL NEVER BE FILLED. A LETHAL COMBINATION IN A LEADER.
> —RON PERLMAN ON TWITTER

At the center of the universe
a hole pulls,
it breaks all bonds
but demands loyalty.

It hates itself almost
as much as it loves itself.

Everything it started
with is ground down to grains,
is grist, is ash, is hunger and it's void.

How can a hole be a heart? Be
an eye? A mouth? A stomach?
An ulcer?

How can it sunder
whomever or whatever it attracts?

It steals all light.
It offers no light.

So many fall into orbit.
So many pledge themselves.
Give
their lives
just to follow.
But there is no where
to go.

The false trail.
Deadend.
Leadless.
Empty.

Souleater.
Friction.
Gravity.
Abyss.
Anti-
Matter

Re-
sist-
ance.

Oracle of Obstruction

I choose the one place
that I might leaf and shade

everyone waits
but I go on being a tree

they stare &
I say *this is not me*

not the me
that I see

Oracle of Collusion

The eye feels

        the jigsaw puzzle piece

    the interlocking of tongue and socket;

            feels dovetails in the air.

Against a horizon of the unsolved

           a flock of blackbirds swirls into the sky

               imitation of a cloud—
this is what we want to believe is happening.

Is this my heart burning or my eye?

    In the ant hive, I see the first portends

        of dulosis.

The mimicry of alarms and war-cries—

in the soul's tv

banners and flags ripple in perfect patriotism

by a false wind.

(We should be happy

that the stock market obliviously bullets through

almost anything—a way to make money is found).

Hunters and gatherers always lack the math skills

in the end, and fall inevitably like the first snow.

There is no match to marching

in orderly rows.

A hive relies on dumb signals: *family, enemy, food,*

PANIC.

To infiltrate is to use the language against itself,

to bombard the workers with propaganda.

To say the word *love* and truly mean it,

as though looking out upon a sea

of faces

all of which are your own.

Preexisting

for days I walk a skeleton

wondering at the body

that has left me—how I might have sloughed off

my entire life

but for the bones

I can wear a robe of sunset

where the star dipping to the horizon

can become my heart

it too is slowly decaying

but I am no threat

except in what was given to me

in strands of code buried in my marrow

even now I can imagine a gate

of bars I cannot slip through

even if I take off a limb

and then another

and slide them through

the arm severed to save the finger

so the old joke goes

I am a gate

and a broken bone-white key

like a raw moon I carry where an organ

might have gone

here beneath my ribs

I have plenty of open air

for which to mark my dreams

with the tombstones of stars

Look where my eyes used to be

listen to the echoes

of myself denying myself

paradise

or earth

I gather my loose bones

my face is a grin

when I feel no joy

no assurances

any ghost can fill me

uncertainty, fear, shame, doom—

haunting molecules and atoms

of ancestry, of history

of being before what may not

live to be tomorrow

Oracle of Confederate Statues

"NOSTALGIA WILL DESTROY CULTURES FASTER THAN
RACISM AND XENOPHOBIA AND SEXISM."
-PATTON OSWALT

"WHAT IS THE FUTURE DOING UNDERNEATH THE PAST?"
-ANNE CARSON

1.
To see the future the eye must burn
must experience its mass in two places
must cross dimensions

must love the flame

No one chooses to see
but not see

no one looks fondly upon the future

2.
What's the use in such knowledge

we have a firm grasp
on myths like old blankets
we wrap ourselves in comfort

let's not read inscriptions
not tonight by the fires
you've carelessly lit

here are the great surrenderers
mounted and pointing stoically
into a battle centuries gone

here once were cannons
and you may still hear the echoes
of the thread-bare and torn dead

and where it should have ended
it did not

These monuments
buried in Ozymandian sand
inscriptions worn
the tired faces warn
men from their hatreds

leave them earthed
and forgotten

now that the world is a better place

3.
you come to me not to see
that which is to come

but here you are
waxing nostalgic over the past

not even your own
but people who died
so long ago their very definition
of human (all humans) should be so different

from your own

4.
Now you fight to continue
to ignore the future
of sand slipping through

whispering truth
does not require your belief
to exist

still, I must open my eyes to this future

whenever yours are closed

There was Time for One More Racial Slur In Ceremony to Honor the Last Code Talkers

"THE MARINES MADE US YELL 'GERONIMO' WHEN WE JUMPED
OUT OF PLANES AND THAT DIDN'T OFFEND ME EITHER."
—THOMAS BEGAY, CODE TALKER

Sometimes you can stand on the top of mesas

and hear true silence

as if you have already slipped away

from your body

left the static voices and machine noises

for pure air.

What the wind says is easy

and so you say nothing

because there is no point.

Sometimes a bad tradition is wrapped

in bad ceremony

and it cannot be over soon enough.

Sometimes the coyotes are in charge.

They call you the names of dead first people,

they think it is an insult—

but it is a reminder that they fear:

something greater was lost than anything gained.

With their Andrew Jackson eyes—

alight with the colors of sunset

and happy for the return to darkness.

They try so hard to be monsters, but they are men,

small-hearted, incapable of surviving

the unblinking star eyes of the desert night.

The Oracle of Tender Shelters

Here is where humanity hums loudest
like an engine of discontent
no matter how much effort is made
to bury this place—
to make it hide.

Here each voice is a siren
calling out across the world to mothers,
mothers and their instinctive hearts—
mothers of the borderless regions
of emotion, mothers who are sirens themselves.

Mothers hear every note of music
and are boundless in their actions,

they are proud of whom they are, they are
citizens in a nation that expands
with every birth.

They hear an anthem play out in every child—
They hear the voice of Nature,
the endless voice of the universe
in every baby, hidden or known.

They look at the tiny borders of men
cutting the land, separating, dividing—
their little hands

trying to control, dominate, drown out, choke
the bonds of family. They love
to hate love. These men love
to hate women. And their children.
These small men, who have forgotten
their own childhood.

These men who have forgotten mothers.

Remember

When your face turned?
You had been so smug
enjoying my fear, taunting me,
See: we're all still here.
I'd repeated the warnings of our elders,
begged you not to elect the match-head president.

Then your face turned as the curtains billowed
as you saw it all go out of control.
All of your faces became the dance of flame light
became the search for exits.

Remember I had to plea with the commandant boy
to cut me loose before shock took over
his body?

You were bawling when the firetrucks arrived.
Later relieved that only the living room and one
bedroom were damaged—my bedroom, of course.
And for the first time I was included
as you explained how we nearly burned
the house down, nearly
died.

But I remember you just had to prove something, you
just had to be right, had to be better,
no matter what.

I still feel the rope burns
on my wrists, the dread for our lives.
Your face twisting with power and control,
till I didn't know you anymore—
you laughed like hell,
holding the box of matches
between us.

Manifestly Unqualified

—CHRIS HAYES

Sometimes Nero's face is lit up so well with fire
that you think this is what a death mask should appear like—
sometimes a scud of rosin clouds rises from bow on strings.
At other moments, there is no music, only Caligula
yelling down the halls, kicking at the air, tiny fists tight
as if he might land a meaningful blow, though this is far
from reality, and the citizenry knows it.
Sometime, the man elected to sit at the prow of the ship,
does not notice the Union dead moaning behind him
as he floats across the Potomac, on his way to Appomattox
to surrender to Robert E. Lee. Somewhere else, an assassin waits
in Ford's Theater just as unable to accept outcomes.
But this president rows onward through his alternative facts,
even as everyone else remembers the right history, the right moment
where muddied field surgeons emerge from tents and add
to the pile of separated limbs that would still, if they could,
kick or punch at the air. Sometimes we are Walt Whitman,
smocked in young blood, broken deep within our hearts,
at what one brother can do to another. Someone else will offer,
Yes, but whatabout..., and the surgeon reaches over
with a freshly amputated arm and says, "Let me stop you,
right there. When this arm held a rifle, it did so to protect
the morals of our Union, not to dismiss all truth so everyone
can get away, or worse yet, rise to a higher level of incompetence."
He tosses the arm, knowing there are more to make a point with inside.
Your haggard Walt spirit will make a small note in your book,
next to a drop of blood that you are unaware of whom it belonged to,
only the cost of how it appeared upon your page.

Oracle of the Wounded Earth

All the dead come forth, out of the mist
out of the smoke

because we cannot stand to live
that close to another

we move out into the fields
into the fuel

and fire marshals fill the air
with words that land like spark and ash

they speak of wind
and calculate energy over area

because our hearts are an open tundra
we do not dream of flames

Shhhh! You do not always hear the mother
                                        breathing, the slow draw

gusts in the scrub brush
sand against itself

I think you see the dead out there ... coming
and you close your eyes

you make up myths about them
how you can kill them before they kill you

still the dead go on accusing
staring through you

and you think if *I believe in a soul*
that would be a thing

to hold or stop them
but the dead wear their blood like clothes

not fashion
not the thing we force to look *natural*

here is where you find the oracle's heart
is a rift, here where it bleeds a river

After School Special (with Armed Teachers)

Mostly, I slept under the bleachers,

even during the games

where conversations settled on the ground

like bubblegum wrappers and the lost

twisties from loosed ponytails.

I heard Mr. Johnson talking to Mr. Williams' wife.

They were going to break the news

they were going to tell him together, like a team

at a prep rally.

Mr. W, who we all made fun of,

because he sweated and had bad breath,

and now I knew something he didn't

about his crappy life.

I smiled bigly.

Dreaming bad-grade revenge,

as the crowds of ghosts cheer for

teams that move up and down but go nowhere.

I tell everyone.

And everyone walks the campus

with knowing, laughing grins,

like deathheads,

like children in the collateral halls,

always moments away from the touch of shadows

and violence.

NATIONALISM

The old man is in the park again
yelling at the welfare fowl
looking for bread
Sad, he says, *Bad geese*
migrating our borders
to take advantage of our system,
to displace american geese.

He wades into hundreds of them
going on about ducks for some reason—
afraid to be seen as afraid
but scared of their magnificent wings,
their flocks, their language.

He says he can build a wall
tall enough to keep them out,
to block the sun for miles,
he says, *the best,*
but no one knows
what it means anymore.

He spreads his arms
like he might fly
or be a false messiah
come to look like he will lead,
but if they follow
it is to the cooking vats—
greasy with the fat of those
who came before—those
looking for a better life
of stale bread and quiet parks;
those who eventually became
american geese.

The Oracle of America First

> "MY PEOPLE JUST HAVE TO HAVE AN ENEMY...
> WE DON'T KNOW WHO WE ARE WITHOUT ONE."
> —A FRIEND ONCE TOLD ME

When my eyes burn a particular red
I can see my neighbor's confederate flag
waving in the wind.

This is a warning to all
that a fear-animal crotches within,
a creature that has found a corner
to back itself into
and will bite.

I envision nazi regalia within
the cave of its house
another flag
what passes for literature
among the bristling furs.
A gun, probably a lugar
or a mauser broomhandle
and kickboots
accompanied by a desire to parade
in a paramilitary fashion.

These creatures
live in a different america
where beneath the waving flag
someone is always stealing
or coveting or wanting to convert them,
push their lives into evolution—
when all they want is to go back, to backup,
back into that a cul de sac
of stale nostalgia.

Their america
needs an enemy within their borders
to blame, to demonize. I knew them,
I knew their victims, I was one.
That old america, never feels right,
with its frightened logic crashing
against its hopes. Those hateful,
trapped animals will blame anything, will
chew off a limb or tear themselves open
looking for the cancer
that is their own hearts.

Oracle of Tribalism

I've seen the body weaponized
those tribal tellers of *truth*
where Cain slaughters Abel
and uses whataboutisms to justify

It doesn't matter whose God
you're dropping a coin in the slot for
anymore—It's all bebop drums
and dog-eat dog-rhythms.

I've seen the constitution weaponized
and the founding fathers
all revolutionary in their poses
and their getups. And no one will ask
a question in church anymore.
No one questions the manufacturing
of scattered bones, wisps of incense,
the manipulated tea leaves
You are required to believe.

I've seen the weaponized world

trust weaponized

love weaponized

I want to say *come back—
Let's sit at the dying campfire
and make new constellations
worthy of our belief.*

But even our ordinary words
have been weaponized.

Oracle of Witch Hunts

Certainly flashlights were burning
into the darkness.
There were whispers,
rumors and lies told—worse, believed!

And the sound of doors
cracking off their frames.

A hive waking—
misdirected, angry, attacking
the shadowed

under the claxons,
under the sirens.
Through the slits of curtains
we saw
people herded into vans,
people cuffed and led away,
people penned,
people executed by revoked asylum.

We saw people treated
as the supernatural beings
rising up from hell.

We saw red light bleed
out over panicked eyes.

The boss of uniforms
said it was him
who was being hunted

but he was doing what all
predators do,
camouflaged and preying

on the helpless
hiding, praying
in the shadows.

Dear Jeff

When you smile your Loki smile, I see
them, you know—all those broken children
in your cages. People whose ancestors came
down through this land following the migratory animal
spirits, while your ancestors were a world away.
In that grimacing grin of yours, Jeff, the untreated
pox-ridden children are weeping and you wear
your bloody executioner's mask, harvesting
the asylum seekers, people so scared
of their deaths in their own countries
that your torture is still a better choice.
What is it about the poor and powerless
that makes you smile like that?
A death-head's grin—do you watch
as they suffer? Are you watching now?
When you tell your lies on TV, do you see
the dying? When I see you coyote
into Congress and claim you can't recall,
are you replaying the dust-choked children
who are crying for their mothers?
Jeff, tell me what the pharoahs sounded like
when they laughed in that bible of yours. Or
what tone the Devil took with Jesus
in the desert? People always assign too much
gravitas to the fallen angel's voice, where I
imagine your voice—a bit ephemeral and effeminate—
insisting within that good book of yours
the cruelty you inflict on the innocent
is something Christ would do.
Jeff, tonight thousands of people are wailing
in your cages, while the guards threaten
and menace in your name, in my name,
in the name of an America I wish you'd never
been born in.

Homunculus

I
will start with my beginning:
I
had no mother...

What she said to me
was *Go win something, anything*

And what
I
found was that it didn't matter if
I
stole or cheated in my returns

it's fine patting my head
and pointed to the exits

I
was my father's child

not some drunken oligarch
of mother's love like my brother

Father showed me

the art of killing for pleasure
especially those who love

unconditionally—

their teary eyes not
understanding how
I
might strangle them

I
loved that
        but not them

Too weak

I
loved myself and no one
could match or beat
that love

Later
I
went on to freeze out
mothers and children who

believe in a fair America

I
hated how they huddled
how they hugged
how they went on and on
loving each other.

I
hollowed skin
and within my shell
the movies of the criminal world

flickered like fire
oily shadows tar-pitted the light

I
extracted fear
and bottled it

then mislabeled it as patriotism.

Who knew

I
could sell the stuff and no
consumer agency came round
looking for ingredients

I
stole a loan from a bank
to build a bottling plant

I
broke my promises
I
broke women into wives
into slaves into children

who worked my factories

I
see great opportunity
I
would say

the workers cheered—
I
stole more from them

And
I
modeled a vision
of a country after black lung

and mortar dust

I
launched a daily dispatch
of accusations and threats

everyone should go to jail
except the loyal
to me

Here in my abandoned nation
of children

with their open carry
bibles, their smoking
guns, and lack of the pre-

existing

everywhere the shadow
flicker of old movies

makes monsters
on our borders

they've all come to work
among us

to take our money
when we aren't watching

and
I
tell the children
only
I
can fix it

and it's true
I
could, but
I
don't
because they would leave

as everyone leaves
as my father and my brother
left

as my never-mother fades
into my uncertainty

into the irreconcilable,
inconsolable pain
of only

I

Adam West

Sometimes I think when a Batman passes away,
all the other Bruce Waynes past and present would attend
the funeral, like heads of state, show respect,
wreathe the grave of the fallen predecessor.

I remember that our superheroes always found a way
to fight the enemies of democracy: Hitler, Mussolini,
Tojo, later Stalin. How they did what was right,
were examples of ideals, standing up for the little guy,
pushing back bullies, and taking the time to care
about community. Said *yes sir,* to the Mayor, or
the Governor, or the Senator, or the President—

without checking their party affiliation first.
Batman never cared about politics except, *May the best,
most qualified person run and win.*
And we'd want to live up to that. Be worthy of such
fairness, such democracy.

Even in the darker knight timelines, the troubled hero still
watched out for his fellow citizen. Cared more for others
than himself, even in his psychic pain he felt his duty—
it grounded him, brought back to good.

So why not, have those actors don their good personas?
Honor the one missing from their fellowship, deliver
eulogies that actually were about their comrade, and didn't
aggrandize their own time in the role or importance.

I guess, why not superheroes—when we've lost
all sense of our leaders.

Fractured Lullaby in a Zinke Landscape

```
"DID I MENTION I'M A GEOLOGIST?"   -OFTEN-TOLD LIE BY RYAN ZINKE
```

Who doesn't look at the mountain   and wonder,
What could that be put to use for?
Who doesn't look where the ancestors are buried,
and wonder   what their time would be like
stuffed   full of chemicals?.

Who doesn't look at the mountain   and think,
How can I break that down for its minerals?
Why wouldn't the spirits   in the water, rocks,
and trees, not want   to be free   of their bonds
and   their   children?

Who doesn't look at the mountain   and ponder,
Where did all this natural resource come from?
Is the spirit energy   trapped in the rocks   not happy
in its home?   Who says, *Granite,   Shale,   Gold,   Ore,
Uranium,*   and thinks   themselves   as liberator or hero?

Who doesn't look at the mountain   and ask,
Could I own this mountain   or sell it?
All the spirits   and ancestors are   thinking
About the government   word,   *relocation,*
And how   much more   the heart   can break?

How to Build a Monster

Remind him every day of his unworthiness.
Compare him to other things you've made
early on. Introduce him to *the bus*—
make sure to throw friends and family
in front of the grill and huge wheels
while he watches, so there is no misunderstanding:
he was built to be, and is, expendable.

Teach him to have contingencies,
especially in relationships.
Try to nail his girlfriends, his wife. Call
it a lesson, or an after-school-special,
even though it is almost certainly
about your own lust.

Tell him little *facts* about the world—
things you've heard but never verified.
Remind him that everyone is part of a conspiracy,
so it's okay to conspire, to collude. Let him
know that he is cosmetically displeasing and needs
augmentation, like your other creations,
he is no natural beauty.

Lead by example: never miss an opportunity
to fart or belch in public, say whatever
comes into your head—don't second guess,
admit nothing, never apologize—
sorry is for losers. Always
keep a fresh harvest of rubes
nearby, to crowd around you,
applaud your every idea and thought. Pay them
if you have to... well, at least promise
to pay them.

Always keep the spawn close, but not
so close as to think you love him.

 Show him how three-card monte
works. Show him how everything
is best when shiny on the surface—
and to run before anyone looks

inside. It's true in real estate, used cars,
and salesmen. Teach him the *dine-and-dash*,
and the *see-you-in-court*. Tell him to hire
people who think they are smarter
than you, then berate them, stiff them,
set them up for *the bus*.

Tell them how great their work is,
Kinda like you, son,
how valued they are,

then it's one good shove
and keep moving
like a shark.

Who Knew?

Deep inside himself the monster is
                                        still puzzled ...

    Who knew?

That national healthcare would be tough.

    Who knew?

You could kill a country with some words made of pixels.

Or nationalism was so divisive.
Or scapegoats would bite back.

Who knew the little girl thrown in the river
wouldn't float like a handful of petals...

shrugging it shambles toward the capitol,

The ghosts of many innocent children in his wake.

The Oracle of Liar, Liar

> "JUST BECAUSE REPORTERS SAY SOMETHING OVER AND OVER AND
> OVER AGAIN DOESN'T START TO MAKE IT TRUE."
> —SARAH HUCKABEE SANDERS

Firstly and for the record,
everything I say is both true
and alternatively true. Yes,
it's in the bible, which is why
we do what we do, even
If proven otherwise. No, I
will not point to the places,
the scriptures, the verses,
to exonerate our actions--just
take my word for it. I baked
all the pies, hours upon hours,
pushing dough into the pan,
I made the filling from scratch—
an old huckleberry recipe. Now
listen, my momma said, I could have
a menfolk job, so long as could bake
and birth ....anyway, my boss always says
what he means, at least, allegorically, at least,
in love. I run through the cities in my firepants,
I say, *there's nothing to see here*, I say, this is all
because of something someone else did.
Look we round up strays fleeing the wreckage—
kids, not our own, but outliers, losers, from another
national anthem—you should be thanking us,
I should be depicted as a saintly heart and halo,
just for standing here every day, answering
the planted questions, beating the weeds
of a fake press—you people, you
never give it a rest, all the little hungry
mouths, opening and closing, chirping,
discontent, I would smother each of you
In my loving arms, hold you
like a borrowed child, and spank
the insolence right off your bottoms.
Did I mention how our love is like a refugee
camp? I would pour hot pie filling
right now, down your open mouths—
daring to ask a question, as you do,

I want to mother you all, *get me a switch,
girl, we'll settle everything right now!*.
I am not your Aunt Lydia, no wait,
I am your Aunt Lydia, only because I
didn't read the book, but I guess I would
be your aunt, if it meant I could discipline you.
I know you'll do your best
to misquote everything I've said, even
if I said it, it'll be out of context.
So here it is:
I looked into all your futures,
cattle cars, camps, some of you are
hobos riding the rails, living near
dumpster fires, dodging detection
and detention, but we will find you all,
my little nieces and nephews,
you can quote me on that!

Landscape with the Fall of Icarus

After everything is all
Splash and spray.
After we cover-up our conspiracy
Hide the evidence
Of our collusion—
How we sent supplies:
Wax, wood, birds, feathers, needles
And threads.
After we went back to working
The good work, god's work—
Herding the sheep,
Plowing the land.

After he'd influenced
And been influenced.
After he flew above the law
But couldn't stop there—
Still wanted more,
Wanted to be the king
Of everything, even of god.

After he was carried out by the tides
We returned to our collective wants
We unfocused our incivility,
Waiting for the next traveling salesman
Who had any easy way out,
The fast cure to the way the world does us—
To all we were born to endure.

"...The Stirring, Unmistakable Patriotism of the Velociraptor..."

There is a guy elected to congress,
who stands in front of everyone
and talks about patriotic dinosaurs
of which (against their lizard brains
and overwhelming hunger) let a human,
the forgotten messiah of his party,
Ronald Reagan, ride upon its back.
The old movie star with crude oil hair
is depicted wielding a machine gun,
with a rocket launcher strapped to his back.
I thought about the victory garden
of irony which is this political party's fruit
and labor. How that early bird ancestor
would become a few drops of gasoline
in the tank of a senator's stretch limousine;
how it and its band of hunters might have eaten
an entire political party if the artist's rendition
had allowed for a time machine. How, the animal
would no doubt choke on our carboned air
if we brought the beast forward to our time,
or even stopped in 1984, to visit the president
and let him ride the blood hungry dino.
Another flower from the irony garden? Reagan
is no doubt firing his machine gun and defending
his United States from all Russian attackers,
something the fantasy-filled senator will forget
next time he votes not to protect our voting systems,
or votes down the sanctions against oligarchs
and their campaign contributions. See, all you young,
impressionable revisionists: history is easy.

YOU WILL
KNOW SMOKE

Autumnal Oracle

At times, I have nearly become a tree
where a branch of dogwood casts its shadow
upon my heart and I can feel the air
change to autumnal dampness, I can
prepare my body for the eventual undressing
and bareness of what is to come,
even as it is colder than remembered,
even as one season begins to dominate.

Still I pledge myself to soil,
each day a renewal of vows—
how else can I awaken and continue?

What I think of as arms are
beginning to curl inward,
starting to call out to the termites'
lust. I tell you, this is not
a sapling's game. You grow
into oldness and you feel
your skin and limbs toughen,
knot up, and sometimes fall
to the earth's own hunger.

There: I've said my daily peace,
I've affirmed both decay and growth.
When I say the word *love*, there
are only empty spaces and sap
behind it. This is what I offer,

for a future,
for salvation
         and damnation.

Oracle of The Late Waking

If you wait until you are awake
then all the changes can be as a surprise—
a horrible nightmare
                      that goes on,
that tears at your chest, claws your leg open
as you try to escape. You think of your family
screaming in the other rooms of your house;
the thumping of boots and bodies being slammed,
the yelling of the beasts many voices
and the lightning searing your eyes,
the thunder tearing further into your flesh.

But you heard everything happening
                                the night before
while so comfortable as to not get out of bed,
    go to the window and watch
        people screaming and crying
            under the talons of colored lights
                which illuminate the roiling clouds above
                      alive live like snakes and eyes—so many eyes!

    All that watching

and the voices of neighbors are replaced
                            with sirens and claxons.

What if you awoke earlier? Followed the unnatural
    sounds, looked out at watchers
    in trench coats, whispering and staring
    into the dark windows of the neighborhood.

        Or if you had gotten up earlier
        seen the telephone repairman on the pole
        in the junction box after normal hours—

    Would you have been suspicious?

Just before you woke,   you struggled with the roaring
    beast outside your window,   the shattering   of doorframes
and windows   next   to your own house.

      Was that a gunshot?   —you were so tired
     from   the interrupting warnings   of the night before
you fluttered   an eye   and closed it   to a melancholy
chambered   music   of your friend   next door's wife
sobbing followed by another   lightning   shot—

and   the orchestra

                        stops

                        playing.

Oracles' End

Truth, like love, has no winners.

This is why you never see
Cassandra at the crap tables
calling out for snake eyes.
The old witches gathered around
the roulette table, their one eye,
bouncing and knocking into one slot
after another, as the wheel slows,
as fate is known.

No, Nostradamus did not catch a ship
to America, never opened a book shop
right off of Main Street. No kids
to legacy. No fortune in untold tales.

And even though there are jail cells,
there's cauldron with bones
that roil and roll from the trick of heroes,
even when the random bullet leaves its war
and finds a collateral skull,

truth, like love, has no losers.

Blind Prophets

In the future
the eyes do not adjust
they see their own smoke.

We are always asking of the blind prophets:

Couldn't you have seen what would happen
to your own eyes?

And if they answer,
it is: *yes*.

Followed by: *what's the use?*

Because you know a thing to happen
you cannot make a thing unhappen.

I feel for your arm, I know where
it will move to.

I know you like to think I see
you going on in your near days
as though I might stop
you and talk, warn, siren, shriek...

But what's the use?

If I cover my eyes,
it is only to protect you—

to keep what I am

held back,

locked in,

not in darkness
but a painful searing light—

one I wish upon
no other set of eyes.

Gacela of Patriotic Traitors

No one doesn't love the rippling snap
of flags bannering and waving, waving
like so many shadows striping your face
like a featherless eagle wanting to fly.

In your dreams, a thousand plastic soldiers
paraded in the capitol with gold-plated dollar signs
emblazed upon their helmets, helmets
of the oceans' enemies and a small heart.

Amidst the ranks and the columns, columns
of the fake salutes your widening shadow
and you talk of the people but you mean
your sad drooping frame in a misfit's suit.

There is false confetti and confessions everywhere,
steaming down the windless streets, the uncomfortable quiet
of Marshall Law, and somewhere, deep within the soul
of this country, the rasp of resistance, resistance.

Oracle of Plutonion

Beneath the tangle of pomegranate branches
trying to reach the moon
I drifted into the valleys of sleep,
near the dead and near dead,
and came to rest beside a small pond.

It's been more than a year that I've been ill
since the first night of visions,
the night that writers were labeled,
Enemies of the State.
And I remembered the words of friends

from totalitarian regimes, who told me
American poets were soft, they'd never been
raided at 3am, taken to a dank cell
and beaten to confess whatever was
in need of a confession.

Too easy to be an American writer
and they all hoped it would stay that way
now that they were granted asylum here..
And I thought about my friends with black sacks
on their heads, cuffed and tossed into vans.

The fear they told me about never knowing
who you'll see or when, ever again. And how
all your notebooks and journals will be gone,
to be used as evidence of your criminal thoughts,
and you will hear each friend say,

Now you will write. Any way you can, you will
write, in your head, on the walls, in dirt,
even sand if you must, you will write,
get one word out, wake the sleeping people—
Write them their anthem.

The Last Vision of Cassandra

there was always something on the horizon

a fleet of ships

Cassandra could see were trouble

and a blood ocean

a departure at dawn—she could see

the burning, the place where dreams

catch a flaming arrow

and reflect their immolation on waves

and when the boiler explodes

a wall in her cell collapses

like genuflecting believers

and she knows this is not escape

just fresh air

gushing ahead of
her own death.

GREAT—AGAIN

Someone who supports the naked
emperor wants me to die
or so he tweets,
and I think of the places
of worship filling up
with bullets,
filling up with flames—
all those houses of god,
all those faces:
god's faces.

If I sleep,
someone's dream
of a border wall built
out of cages
haunts me.
Each cage is a group
of children
a chorus of babies
claxon into the desert wind.
Their faces are caked with dirt
and tears. And I say,
God's faces.

Their parents gone.
My parents are gone too,
lucky to have died believing
in our better country,
where our ancestors died
fighting against dictators
and imperialists.
I remember the story
of my great uncle
burning in the Pacific.

I think of the reservations
that became internment camps—
good citizens kept
in pens for being a color,
for being immigrants.
In my American dream,

a bomb pushes everything
away for miles
and turns the sand to glass.

Tonight the emperor is doing
a slight of hand—
an invisible 3-card Monty,
he tells us each card is
like a stealth fighter.
He says, *just trust me,*
everybody's a winner!
He looks at us in the eye
and demands, *Tell me*
what you want to hear.
He throws an invisible ball
into the air, some us look
where there is nothing,
I watch him fill his pockets
with cash. *Everybody's a winner!*
if you can believe
he's wearing clothes.

Oracle of Recurring Oracles

> "THEN THEY CAME FOR ME..."
> —MARTIN NIEMÖLLER

We like to say the lesson has been learned,
we'll never make that mistake, again.
There are echoes all the way down history:
Will never happen here.
                      And then happens here.

The charismatic will say whatever you want to hear.
        They love the past, they want to take you to the past.
                The past is death. All of it.
The moment is gone.
                      The people are gone.
                      The part of us that came from the past
                      is dead cells ready to slough.
        The charismatic love death.
                They will always bring you to it.
                What did you want? A stagnant world? An old job?
                Something lost but not really had?
                      Death loves nostalgia. Death loves the past.

One night there is a quiet harvest moon watchful
over our lands, the next:
                Bonfires. Book burnings.
A whole state's white population deputized:
permitted to storm the houses of black families to take guns.
                                      TAKE GUNS!!!
Or a whole side of a city goes to burn the other side.
Or people, hundreds of people, disappear.
                                    No one asking of them. Just
                sudden migrations. All possessions left behind.
        Who are the immigrants? Who are different? Who live behind fences now?
            Who were the interned, stacked on the reserved?
                Who were scrubbed from their lands? Their rights?
Who still believes in justice?

Now paramilitaries under a starless sky.
        Lists are made.
        Lists are the last remembrances.
        Lists of enemies.
        Lists of probable resisters.

Lists of journalists.
Lists of party members.
Lists of the comedians.
Lists of the activists.
Lists of leaders.
Lists of artists.

Lists of oracles.

They are kept divided.
Under the banners and flags of false patriotism
    people are hunted,
        the old anthems are being sung
            by the blue light praises on State TV.

    Everyone relies far too much on time.
        If we wait long enough...
        Someone will save us...
        Another country will fight for us...
        It's what we used to do...
        Maybe the dictator will die...
Time is a history lesson. Time is never a friend.

        Even now, you hear gasoline tossed out of a can.

            You hear matchsticks marching

                ...and do nothing.

How many ghosts regret they did nothing while alive?

How many regrets echo in time?

        Yes, even as you hate me for my sight,

        even as they take me away from your sight,

you will know smoke

and you will know what it means.

                    This is my prophecy.

                          This is my body burning

                                this is the ashes

                                          powdering your face ghost gray

                                          moments before your own end.

Acknowledgments

The author expresses his gratitude to the editors of the following magazines for publishing earlier versions of poems within this book:

Poetry 24: "'...The Stirring, Unmistakable Patriotism of the Velociraptor...'"; "Great—Again"

diode: "Oracle of Liar, Liar"; "Rural Oracles"; "Oracle of Inward Vision"; "Preexisting"

Califragile: "Oracle of Confederate States"; "Oracle of Collusion"; "Oracle's End"; "The Oracle of Warranties"; "Oracle of Witch Hunts"; "Fractured Lullaby in a Zinke Landscape"

American Journal of Poetry: "Homunculus"; "How to Build a Monster"; "After School Special (with Armed Teachers)"

Good Works Review: "Oracle of Rust"; "Oracle of the Virga Fields"; "Oracles of Vanity"

Collateral Damage: "Dear Jeff"; "Oracle of the Tender Shelters"

The author also expresses gratitude to Ami Kaye and Steven Asmussen and the entire staff of Glass Lyre Press.

Glass Lyre Press

exceptional works to replenish the spirit

Glass Lyre Press is an independent literary publisher interested in technically accomplished, stylistically distinct, and original work. Glass Lyre seeks diverse writers that possess a dynamic aesthetic and an ability to emotionally and intellectually engage a wide audience of readers.

Glass Lyre's vision is to connect the world through language and art. We hope to expand the scope of poetry and short fiction for the general reader through exceptionally well-written books, which evoke emotion, provide insight, and resonate with the human spirit.

Poetry Collections
Poetry Chapbooks
Select Short & Flash Fiction
Anthologies

www.GlassLyrePress.com

www.ingramcontent.com/pod-product-compliance
Lightning Source LLC
Chambersburg PA
CBHW020125130526
44591CB00032B/530